The Light
Within

The Light Within

Fiona Gobin

THE LIGHT WITHIN

Scripture taken from The Holy Bible, King James Version. Public Domain

iUniverse books may be ordered through booksellers or by contacting:

iUniverse
1663 Liberty Drive
Bloomington, IN 47403
www.iuniverse.com
844-349-9409

ISBN: 978-1-6632-2980-9 (sc)
ISBN: 978-1-6632-2981-6 (e)

Library of Congress Control Number: 2021920128

Print information available on the last page.

iUniverse rev. date: 10/07/2021

The true author of this book
Is Yahweh, God Almighty.
I am just the messenger
Who penned the words
He brought me.
—Fiona

Acknowledgements

I wish to express profound gratitude to my family, my parents, and my aunt for their support. I hope they enjoy reading my book.

Special thanks to my childhood friend Navindra for being an inspiration during my dark days. He was there from the first pen stroke and listened attentively to my drafts.

Heartfelt thanks to my book editor, Ms Sapphira La Mothe, and my cover designer, Mr Ephraim La Mothe of B Wired Consultancy Services.

Sincere gratitude to my publisher, iUniverse, for the tremendous job they did of making my book a success.

Thanks to Prophetic Encounter Team for their prayers.

Unless otherwise noted, all quotations come from the Holy Bible, New King James Version.

Behold, God is my salvation; I will trust and not be afraid: for the LORD JEHOVAH is my strength and my song; he also is become my salvation.

—Isaiah 12:2

Introduction

That God of our Lord Jesus Christ, the Father
of glory, may give unto you the spirit of
wisdom and revelation in the knowledge of
him: the eyes of your understanding being
enlightened; that ye may know what is the
hope of his calling, and what the riches of the
glory of his inheritance in the saints, and what
is the exceeding greatness of his power to us-
ward who believe, according to the working of
his mighty power.

(Ephesians 1:17–19)

I wrote this book during a tumultuous time in my life
where the hand of God was evident. It was during these
dark days that I found the light within, and I pray these
words will illuminate your life and in so doing help you
find your light within.

Life is a precious gift and should not be wasted. It
is priceless beyond the finest tags of gold and ornate
jewellery. It is vitally important that we be thankful for
all the blessings we receive.

God's loving-kindness and tender mercies are new every day. The breath of fresh air, the sunlight, the rainfall that replenishes the earth—all denote the glory and wondrous works of our Lord.

See the goodness that surrounds you. Look within and recognise the beauty that exists. Then you can truly appreciate so many things and people in your life.

Each day is an opportunity to fulfil your purpose, that is, your God-given destiny that was birthed before you were born. It equips you with confidence to forge ahead and brings you the profound joy in finding your identity. To discover your purpose, you have to listen to the small voice within that speaks and directs you.

There is a light that radiates from within to help each of us on our journey. It is your inner strength. When you find your inner strength, you are able to fulfil your purpose. Choose to step out and shine. Embrace each day with gratitude. Be resilient and have perseverance, willpower, and self-control. Possess courage. Have an inner strength that initiates inner peace, forgiveness, healing, and restoration.

This light glows when you are spiritually grounded. Reading God's word and meditating on it regularly builds your inner strength.

So you must be persistent in prayer and unwavering in worship and meditation.

> The Lord is my light and my salvation; whom shall I fear? the Lord is the strength of my life; of whom shall I be afraid?
>
> (Psalm 27:1)

Inner Strength

I can do all things through Christ Jesus who strengthens me.

(Philippians 4:13)

Life is a series of challenges that daily we overcome. Overcoming releases an inner strength. Sometimes you are unaware of the strength you possess, until being strong is the only way forward through turmoil and agony.

Life allows hurt so you can become a better version of yourself. It brings about retrospect and causes self-evaluation to find your true purpose. It also presents itself to reveal your hidden potential, explore the very essence of your being, by reaching into the recesses of your heart.

Inner strength helps you to be grounded in the face of adversity. When there is chaos all around, let the light within illuminate your path. No matter what battle you face, inner strength enables you to stand steadfast. "Trust ye in the Lord for ever: for in the Lord Jehovah is everlasting strength" (Isaiah 26:4).

When you are in a dark place mentally, allow that light to shine. Trials are temporary, so be encouraged to rise above life's challenges and overcome them.

When you feel like you cannot continue, remember there is light at the end of the tunnel. Situations come and situations go, but the person looking at you in the mirror is the one who has to grow psychologically, spiritually, and emotionally.

Inner strength can be developed when you surrender all to God and place your trust in Him. Spending time with Him builds your inner strength. When difficulties come, let your inner strength and faith sustain you.

Always keep these faithful words in your heart: "Fear thou not; for I am with thee: be not dismayed; for I am thy God: I will strengthen thee; yea, I will help thee; yea, I will uphold thee with the right hand of my righteousness" (Isaiah 41:10).

From the Bible, we learn that Joseph was tested several times. He was put in a pit by his brothers and then sold to the Ishmaelites; he was also falsely accused and imprisoned.

He was able to overcome adversity by his brothers and Potiphar's wife. He was not rebellious and did not yield to temptation. He displayed exemplary inner strength. He was a noble character. While he was facing his own storms, he assisted others.

Sometimes when you are facing your own storms in life, your strength is tested by helping others deal with their own battles. Never be so overwhelmed by your trials that you turn a blind eye to someone else's cry for help.

Joseph's faith and trust in God delivered him. He was being prepared and positioned for that great role God had for him. Joseph interpreted the dreams of the butler and the baker while in prison. He simply could have remained silent upon hearing their dreams.

However, that was the initial stage in the fulfilment of his purpose. By doing this, he was eventually remembered by the butler when Pharoah had dreams that no one in Egypt could have interpreted. He was called before Pharoah to interpret and was rewarded by becoming the governor of Egypt.

Be a lifeboat, be a pillar of strength to others. Be genuine and kind. The greatest struggle brings about the greatest blessings.

King David also displayed inner strength when Israel was invaded by the Amalekites and took the women and children. The people wanted to stone him for this. However, David called upon God for advice and was instructed what to do.

The lesson for us is when we are in times of distress and uncertainty, we should seek God's guidance. Tap into your inner strength through prayer. God will guide you. By meditation, singing psalms, and playing the harp, David built his inner strength.

Samson, a man who had great physical strength but not inner strength, yielded to temptation. He disclosed the secret of his power, his hair. This eventually destroyed him. So we see that having physical strength but lacking inner strength can cause our downfall.

Prayer for Inner Strength

Almighty Father,
I know at times
I am weak,
And I am overwhelmed
With fears and anxiety.
I rest all my cares
At Your feet.
I pray
For Your strength
To uphold me each day.
For in You I live and move
And have my being.
In Jesus's name I pray.

Amen.

Resilience

> Trust in the Lord with all thine heart; and lean
> not unto thine own understanding. In all thy
> ways acknowledge Him and He shall direct
> thy paths.
>
> (Proverbs 3:5–6)

Resilience is the ability to bounce back to normal after facing tough situations. It is being able to cope mentally and emotionally, to be strong or even stronger than before.

Being optimistic and having a positive attitude are the foundations for healthy, wholesome emotions. These are also the contributing factors for resilience.

It is not always easy being resilient. However, consistent communication with God and building a relationship with Him through difficult moments allow you to dust yourself off, pick up the pieces, and be an overcomer.

When you are faced with storms and distresses always keep focused on God. He never gives up on you. Always be mindful that God is near no matter the situation.

When you are resilient, you are able to continue moving forward. Difficulties and challenges make you stronger.

Although at times you may feel your burdens are too much to carry, God does not allow more than you can bear. Whatever battles you face, remember it belongs to God Almighty. He also uses ways to prepare His soldiers for their purpose and calling.

A prime example of resilience in the Bible is Moses. He was chosen to lead the children of Israel out of Egypt where they were slaves. He encountered many challenges and disappointments. He faced harsh criticisms and discontentment from the Israelites.

However, in his leadership role, he disobeyed God by striking the rock twice for water. His disobedience resulted in him not being able to enter the Promised Land. He was able to see it from afar but not enter. God never reneges on His words.

Although disheartened by his grave mistake, Moses still carried the mantle and led the people. This proved him to be resilient even when he was disappointed. He rose above that, dusted himself, and moved ahead. We see here that being strong is sometimes the only way forward.

"But they that wait upon the Lord shall renew their strength; they shall mount up with wings as eagles; they shall run, and not be weary; and they shall walk, and not faint" (Isaiah 40:31).

Another character in the Bible of marked resilience is Ruth. She can be referred to as the pillar of hope and tenacity. She and her mother-in-law, Naomi, suffered the death of their husbands. Naomi suffered the loss of both her sons as well.

They faced grief, sadness, tragedy, and famine. However, Ruth was steadfastly minded or strong willed. She was resolute in her decision to stay with her mother-in-law. This is evident when she said, "Whither thou goest, I will go; and where thou lodgest, I will lodge: thy people shall be my people, and thy God my God: Where thou diest, will I die and there will I be buried: the Lord do so to me, and more also, if ought but death part thee and me" (Ruth 1:16-17).

Ruth was determined to look after Naomi even if it meant going into a strange land. She did not give up or wallowed in her sorrow. She took to the fields to get food for their survival.

Although they faced tragedy and loss, Ruth intended to make life better for them. She displayed great resilience by overcoming the hurdles in her life and was geared towards improvement.

Her resilience brought her blessings, restoration, and purpose in life. She got married to the owner of the field, Boaz, a relative of her deceased father-in-law.

This union produced a son called Obed from whom the Lord Jesus Christ descended. Throughout Ruth's life, we see God was orchestrating His plan for her purpose to be fulfilled. Ruth's resilience, her ability to bounce back from tragedy and suffering are lessons for us to learn. So when we are sometimes discouraged by the difficulties we face, it should be remembered God is in the midst.

"And we know that all things work together for good to them that love God, to them who are called according to His purpose" (Romans 8:28).

Esther, or Hadassah, is another character of striking resilience. She was an orphaned Jewish girl who was raised by her uncle Mordecai. There was no female figure in her life to guide her. She did not bemoan about her loss and did not give in to self-pity. However, she was thrust into palace life whilst being a captive. After Queen Vashti was banished for her disobedience, Esther found favour in the eyes of the king and subsequently became queen.

She saved the lives of the king, her uncle Mordecai, and her people. Her requests unto the king were never denied. Her faith in God gave her the strength and courage she needed. God was upholding her and taking charge of her life. She was fulfilling the purpose God had for her.

She revealed the deceitful plan of his top aid, Haman, to have all the Jewish people killed who were captives in Sushan. The king acted on this and sentenced Haman to be hanged.

Esther could have been put to death as well for this request to save her people and for hiding her identity, which was revealed only at that time. However, her faith in God steered her through it. She rose from being a young, shy girl to a woman of action, mission, persistence, faith, and resilience.

Esther means *star*, and rightly so, she was the one who illuminated the lives of the Jewish people. She fulfilled her purpose to save and protect them.

"Have not I commanded thee? Be strong and of a good courage; be not afraid, neither be thou dismayed: for the Lord thy God is with thee withersoever thou goest" (Joshua 1:9).

Prayer for Resilience

Great and mighty God,
Creator and sustainer of all things,
Father, I seek
Your divine assistance
That I may be able to rise
Above all obstacles.
When challenges
Come my way, Lord
I pray
That I will be able
To overcome.
May Your grace be sufficient
To see me through,
To bring me to the perpetual light
Of Your hope and mercy
In Jesus's most holy name, I pray.

Amen.

Willpower

For God hath not given us the spirit of fear:
but of power, and of love, and of a sound mind.

(2 Timothy 1:7)

Willpower is having determination, strength of mind, self-discipline, and self-control. It comes from within and is a factor of inner strength.

Tapping into willpower enables you to handle stressful situations and resist temptations. It allows you to maximise your potential and achieve your life's goals.

Stressful situations are no doubt part of life, however the way in which they are confronted or handled say much. You either add fuel or neutralise it. Having willpower allows you to deal with situations in a more subtle and delicate way.

Willpower is the driving force to achieve success. It is having the determination to reach the pinnacle of greatness. When you possess this, nothing can deter you from being the best you can be. It enables you to strive for excellence and fulfil your life's purpose. It is having determination to overcome difficulties and challenges.

Self-control is the ability to control your emotions and desires when you are faced with temptations. Having self-control is important so you do not become controlled by the desires of the world. The Bible is a medium for achieving self-control by meditating on the words.

In 1 Samuel 24, we can see that David exercised great self-control by sparing Saul's life. Although Saul was after David's life and David was in hiding, he had the opportunity to kill Saul in the cave where he and his men hid.

However, David surreptitiously creeps up on Saul and cuts piece of his robe to prove to Saul how easily he could have been killed. David knew Saul was God's appointed king of Israel, so he allowed him to live.

Also, we can learn an amazing lesson of self-control from the Lord Jesus Christ while He was fasting in the wilderness. He resisted temptation and overcame the situation by tapping into willpower, determination, self-control, and self-discipline.

Self-discipline is a way of training yourself to make improvements in your life. It helps you to be focused so you can achieve your goals.

Self-discipline is being able to motivate yourself. It grooms you to be patient and understanding. It helps you stand against negative and bad influence. Self-discipline removes distraction.

Prayer for Willpower

Most merciful
Father in heaven,
I humbly come before You
Seeking Your guidance
To achieve willpower,
Self-control, and self-discipline.
At times I may fail, Lord,
But I rely on You
To place me on the right path
That I may serve You
In the way You want me to.
Hear my prayer
In the blessed name of Jesus,
Our Saviour.

Amen.

Perseverance

And not only so, but we glory in tribulations also: knowing that tribulation worketh patience; and patience, experience; and experience, hope: and hope maketh not ashamed; because the love of God is shed abroad in our hearts by the Holy Spirit which is given unto us.

(Romans 5:3–5)

Perseverance is the ability to continue despite obstacles, to keep you going in order to better yourself, to accomplish your goals and fulfil your purpose. Struggles are present in life's journey, but to overcome, you must persevere.

Perseverance is a component of inner strength. No matter what life throws at you, keep moving forward. At times you may feel that your strength is insufficient, but look within, and our Father in heaven will provide the courage to propel you.

Even though you may encounter failure, you will realise that it is the stepping stone to achieve your goals. With the right attitude, you must keep trying.

When one door closes, there are other doors opened to become successful. However, we stare too long at the closed door that we are unable to see the breakthrough just before us.

Perseverance is having a positive mindset. Always be optimistic in life to become a better version of yourself and fulfil your purpose.

Just like a mountain climber who is ardent in his pursuit, he suffers many falls, bruises, and setbacks to arrive at the top of the mountain. Despite these, he perseveres because he knows victory and success await him. After all the struggles, it is worth it because perseverance brings glory and the feeling of contentment. You must not give up.

There is so much to discern from the character of Job in the Bible. He was an upright man; he feared God and shunned evil. He had seven sons and three daughters. He owned seven thousand sheep, three thousand camels, five hundred yoke of oxen, five hundred donkeys, and a large number of servants. He was the greatest man among all the East. He possessed wealth in abundance.

However, he lost his possessions and children. He endured immense suffering but never gave up. His faith in God sustained him. He persevered through all his sufferings.

Job's grief and losses were compounded by him being inflicted with boils, however he continued despite all the obstacles he faced. It implies a great lesson for us that we must trust God even when we are unaware of what is going on.

Job's wife advised him to curse God and die, but he quickly rebuked her for such utterance. He showed faith and strength in doing so.

Throughout these encounters, Job proved his faithfulness to God, patience, and extraordinary perseverance. As a result of this, he was blessed more in the later part of his life.

We can also learn that while we serve God and have our hearts' desires, trials and tribulations will come to test us.

To summarise, we see that the tribulations we face make us stronger and strengthen our faith in God. Even when we are uncertain, we must persevere and find the courage within to continue, and God will do the rest. Trust God in all seasons of life.

Another character of unwavering perseverance is Hannah, which aptly means "favour". She was the wife of Elkanah. Hannah was provoked because of her barrenness. She took her grievances to God in prayer while she endured this. In her bitterness, she prayed to God and made her request for a son, whom she vowed to give to God. She persevered despite being ridiculed.

She continued unfalteringly and sought God all the more. She trusted in God's timing and displayed patience, faith, and perseverance just like Job. Her persistence in prayer was once mistaken by the priest Eli for drunkenness. Her lips moved, but no words were heard.

However, the words emitted from the depths of her heart. She never became weary of speaking to God. The provocation she faced brought her closer to Him.

Eli the priest bade her peace and God's fulfilment of her request. This certainly comforted her because she believed it would come true.

As a result of this, she received God's favour, the true meaning of her name. Her prayer was answered, and she was given a son, Samuel, which means "Asked of God". Through faith, loyalty, and persistence in prayer, she was able to reap her reward.

When obstacles come your way, you must reach into the recesses of your inner being and find the strength to go on. Let God guide you.

It should also be remembered that when you pray wholeheartedly, God listens and answers. It is imperative to honour your vows when you receive the answer to your prayers. Be thankful unto Him.

Hannah did not forget her vow, and she exalted God with a powerful song of thanksgiving. She gave back her son to God, who became a great prophet in Israel.

So when you are faced with the storms of life just like Job and Hannah, be confident you will overcome through faith, patience, perseverance—and with Almighty God by your side.

"Praying always with all prayer and supplication in the Spirit, and watching thereunto with all perseverance and supplication" (Ephesians 6:18).

Prayer for Perseverance

Gracious,
Ever–loving Father,
I pray for
Perseverance
To go on.
Trusting in You, Lord,
Will equip me
With the faith I need
To endure any situation.
For You are a shield
And a rock.
May You continue
To be my guide,
My sustainer,
And my deliverer
In the powerful name
Of Jesus.

Amen.

Inner Peace

Therefore being justified by faith, we have
peace with God through our Lord Jesus Christ:
by whom also we have access by faith into his
grace wherein we stand, and rejoice in hope of
the glory of God.

(Romans 5:1–2)

Inner peace is obtained when you are satisfied with your
identity. That is who you are and what you are about. It
is accepting every detail of your life and where you are
in life's journey.

Inner peace allows transition to a meaningful and
purposeful life. It declutters the mind of all negativity.
It prevents negative emotions from taking root. It is a
barrier to protect the serene state of mind. It helps you to
be composed in times of difficulty.

Inner peace brings you into an entirely different realm
of mindfulness and positivity. It aligns you with your
life's purpose. Inner peace brings out the beauty within.
When you experience this, you are at peace with the

world around you. You are able to live harmoniously with others. It also promotes forgiveness.

Inner peace removes fears, worry, and anxiety. It contributes to mental, physical, and emotional equilibrium. It encourages spiritual and psychological growth.

This characteristic of inner strength brings calm to your entire body. It is when the body and mind are in harmony. It is the soothing balm to heal all internal wounds.

Inner peace is the antidote for emotional and psychological trauma. It is beneficial to physical health and well-being. Inner peace reduces stress and allows you to better deal with situations that may arise.

It replenishes and restores. Inner peace resuscitates so you can enjoy the precious gift of life which God has given to you.

Inner peace is also the state of experiencing spiritual serenity. This is achieved by nurturing your mind through prayer and meditation, establishing a relationship with the Creator, who is also called the God of Peace.

"Thou wilt keep him in perfect peace, whose mind is stayed on thee: because he trusteth in thee" (Isaiah 26:3).

Inner peace comes by building your faith in God. It is having belief and trust in His words. When a situation arises, rest assured that God will take care of it.

By opening your heart and allowing God to take control of your life, you are stepping into inner peace. When this is done, you dismiss yourself from ill thoughts and emotions.

"And the peace of God, which passeth all understanding, shall keep your hearts and minds through Christ Jesus" (Philippians 4:7).

God loves to hear from you and wants you to be happy. Inner peace is the source of happiness, contentment and joy. You were not created to be distressed or unhappy.

However, during times of sorrow, leaning on Him provides inner peace and comfort. His presence in your life means you are better prepared to handle any unforeseen circumstances.

The epitome of inner peace is our heavenly Father. He is also the Author of Peace. He creates and delivers it. He is slow to anger, which shows the peacefulness of His character. He also wants us to seek peace and pursue it.

> The Lord is gracious and full of compassion;
> slow to anger and of great mercy.
>
> The Lord is good to all: and his tender mercies
> are over all his works.
>
> (Psalm 145:8–9)

In Judges 6, the children of Israel did evil, and God delivered them into the hands of the Midianites. They were greatly impoverished because of their wicked ways. They cried unto God, who eventually sought to deliver them.

An angel appeared unto Gideon, a man of valour, and outlined the task ahead. Gideon asked for a sign to indicate it was God who spoke to him. The angel instructed him to offer a sacrifice with a kid and unleavened cakes. Then he laid them upon a rock in Ophrah. Broth was poured over, and then a fire consumed it, which revealed this was done by God. It was the sign for Gideon.

The Lord said unto him, "Peace be unto thee; fear not: thou shalt not die."

Afterwards, Gideon built an altar there unto the Lord and called it Jehovah-Shalom, which means "The Lord is Peace". So suffice it to say that God is indubitably the God of Peace.

The other character of notable peace is the Lord Jesus Christ. Through Him we are able to achieve complete inner peace in our lives. Before His birth, He was acclaimed as the Prince of Peace.

"For unto us a child is born, unto us a son is given: and the government shall be upon his shoulder: and his name shall be called Wonderful, Counsellor, The mighty God, The everlasting Father, The Prince of Peace" (Isaiah 9:6).

When He was born, praise resounded, which meant that He was the one who brought peace for everyone and the world.

"Glory to God in the highest, and on earth peace, good will toward men" (Luke 2:14).

The Lord Jesus urged His disciples to love their enemies, do good, and bless and pray for those who used and persecuted them.

In John 14:27, He offers these comforting words: "Peace I leave with you; my peace I give unto you: not as the world giveth, I give unto you. Let not your heart be troubled, neither let it be afraid."

21

Prayer for Inner Peace

Heavenly Father,
I ask for Your peace, which
Surpasseth all understanding.
I pray that my thoughts
Are fixed on You alone.
Let my mind and heart
Be at rest in You.
Inner peace can only
Come from You
Through our Lord Jesus.
May You continue
To be my comfort
In Jesus's precious name.

Amen.

Forgiveness

And be ye kind to one another, tenderhearted,
forgiving one another, even as God for Christ's
sake hath forgiven you.

(Ephesians 4:32)

Forgiveness is pardoning someone for the hurt or agony
they caused you. It is when you choose to leave those
painful emotions behind and not hold them against that
person. It is not harbouring anger, bitterness, grudges,
or negative thoughts anymore. It is not seeking revenge.

It is wise to forgive before it is too late. Make peace
with your past because that will remove the shackles of
hurt and animosity. When you make peace with your past
and yourself, only then you can set yourself free. You do
not have to carry these feelings into the future.

Forgiveness is like a heavy burden lifted off your
shoulders when you allow it. When you let go, then you
grow.

You are able to detach yourself from the negative
emotions that have been weighing you down. Forgiveness

allows you to spread your wings and fly, to soar to unbelievable heights.

It helps you recognise your identity and enables you to fulfil your purpose without hindrances. Forgiveness empowers you to step into a different stage in your life. It closes the door to your past and opens a new one.

When you experience one bad chapter in your life that is not the end of your story. Flip the page and read on. Better things await you.

Forgiveness instils peace and brings healing and restoration. It fosters positive emotions which are healthy for you.

Never wish ill to anyone. So forgive, live, and let live. Our God is full of mercy and forgiveness and desires the same from us. If He can forgive us our iniquities, then who are we to not forgive?

"Forbearing one another, and forgiving one another, if any man have a quarrel against any: even as Christ forgave you, so also do ye" (Colossians 3:13).

Forgive

Forgive
Those who
Have done you wrong.
You will overcome;
You are strong.
Let that burden be behind you.
There is joy on the horizon.
Start your life anew.
Let your heart heal from pain.
Give it to God;
He will make it whole again.
Let peace
Reign in your mind.
So forgive others and be kind.
When you forgive,
You grow.
Then the blessings will flow
Which God has in store for you.

We see God's forgiveness at many instances in the Bible. The people who were called by God to serve committed grave mistakes, but when they asked God for forgiveness, they were forgiven. Asking for forgiveness is not all there is to it, but when you ask it from your heart, then God really forgives.

Moses, the great leader, also committed a sinful act. He witnessed an Egyptian beating an Israelite, which enraged him. He took the matter into his own hands and slew that Egyptian.

This was punishable because he had committed murder. God sees all and was aware of this, but He forgave Moses because he was the one to lead His people out of Egypt. That was the purpose Moses had to fulfil.

> Now therefore, behold, the cry of the children of Israel is come unto me: and I have also seen the oppression wherewith the Egyptians oppress them.
>
> Come now therefore, and I will send thee unto Pharoah, that thou mayest bring forth my people the children of Israel out of Egypt.
>
> (Exodus 3:9–10)

Another person who was forgiven by God is Jonah. He was instructed to go to the city of Nineveh and preach repentance to the people. Instead, he disobeyed and fled to Tarshish by ship, thinking he could hide from God.

However, this act brought God's displeasure, and a storm arose in the sea. Jonah was asleep, but the others cast lots, and it fell on him, indicating he was responsible for the storm. He also revealed to them that he had fled from God's presence. Jonah requested they throw him into the sea to bring calm. He was thrown overboard, and a large fish sent by God swallowed him.

In Jonah 2, Jonah cried unto God to save him. He meticulously described his harrowing experience when he was thrown into the sea. God heard his prayers and allowed the large fish to spill him out.

God showed his forgiveness here, and Jonah fulfilled his purpose by going to Nineveh and doing what God called him to do: warn the people about the destruction of their city if they did not repent.

The people of Nineveh were also forgiven by God because they turned from their wicked ways. They obeyed his voice through Jonah, and God was very pleased with this. When God sees our changed behaviour, He forgives.

King David who was a little shepherd boy, the last of seven sons, and he became king over Israel. He was a man after God's own heart. He was specifically chosen by God to rule Israel and fulfil his purpose.

However, he made many mistakes during the tenure of his kingship. He committed murder, and he disobeyed God by having a census of the population, which he was warned not to do by Joab. He also committed adultery. He suffered many tragedies, and the people of Israel and his own family suffered as a result of his mistakes.

The relationship between his family members was far from perfect. One of his sons raped his daughter, and the other killed him. It all stemmed from the punishment God passed upon King David for his sins.

In Psalm 51, David poured out his heart before God, showing how remorseful he was for committing adultery.

> Have mercy upon me, O God, according to thy lovingkindness: according unto the multitude of thy tender mercies blot out my transgressions.

> Wash me thoroughly from mine iniquity, and cleanse me from my sin.

> For I acknowledge my transgressions: and my sin is ever before me.

(Psalm 51:1–3)

David pleaded to God for forgiveness and was forgiven. His purpose was also fulfilled and God established a covenant with him (2 Samuel 7:12–16) that outlined the following: That He would give a son to him who would build a house for God's name, although David desired to build it. He would establish the throne of his kingdom forever. That son was King Solomon, who fulfilled his part of the covenant after David died.

David's house and kingdom would be established forever before him; his throne would be established forever.

This covenant shed light on the lineage of the Lord Jesus Christ, the future King. He descended from King David, royal blood. He was the true Son referred to, and His kingdom to come would be everlasting.

David's prayer of thanksgiving after hearing of this covenant elucidated his relationship with the Creator. He acknowledged that it was God who did all the great things in his life. He magnified, glorified, and blessed Him for all his goodness.

"Wherefore thou art great, O Lord God: for there is none like thee, neither is there any God beside thee, according to all that we have heard with our ears" (2 Samuel 7:22).

David was a poet, musician, and psalmist. His famous Psalm 23 expounds on trusting God in all seasons of life. It speaks about God's mighty hand over his life. He guides, provides, protects, disciplines, forgives, heals, restores, and blesses.

Psalm 23

The Lord is my shepherd; I shall not want
[Guide and Provider]
He maketh me to lie down in green pastures:
[He gives rest]
He leadeth me beside still waters
[Refreshes]
He restoreth my soul
[Brings healing]
He leadeth me in the paths of righteousness
[He shows the right way]
For His name's sake
[His purpose to fulfil]
Yea, though I walk through the valley
of the shadow of death
[In trials]

I will fear no evil: for thou art with me
[Protector and Faithful]
Thy rod and staff they comfort me
[Correction]
Thou preparest a table before me
In the presence of mine enemies
[Safety]
Thou anointest my head with oil
([Prosperity]
My cup runneth over
[Abundance]
Surely goodness and mercy shall follow me
All the days of my life
[Blessings]
And I will dwell in the house of the Lord forever.
[Always in God's presence]

Saul, renamed Paul, was another biblical character who was forgiven by God. He persecuted the Christians in Jerusalem; he created havoc of the church, entered into every house, and took men and women to prison.

He sent out threats and slaughtered the disciples of the Lord. He went to the high priest and desired to have letters sent to the synagogues in Damascus indicating that if any Christian was found that way, they would be captured and brought to Jerusalem.

However, while on his journey to Damascus, a bright light shone about him, and he became blind. The Lord Jesus questioned why He was being persecuted. The Lord Jesus identified Himself and gave instruction to Saul.

Saul was led by his men into Damascus because he was blind. For three days, he was blind and consumed nothing. The disciple Ananias was called by God to visit Saul and pray for his sight. Ananias was reluctant at first because he knew of Saul's persecution of the Christians.

> But the Lord said unto him, Go thy way: for he is a chosen vessel unto me, to bear my name before the Gentiles, and kings, and the children of Israel:
>
> For I will shew him how great things he must suffer for my name's sake.
>
> (Acts 9:15–16)

Ananias went to Saul and prayed for his sight to return. He received his sight and was baptised. From then on, he preached about Christ along with the disciples.

So again we discern that God had forgiven him despite his persecutions against the Christians. His plan for Paul's life was opposite of what he did. Paul obeyed and fulfilled his purpose.

The Lord Jesus Christ also showed forgiveness when He was on the cross. Here was an innocent man who had committed no crime or wrongdoing but was being punished and facing death. He never complained or rebelled. We all know He was subjected to this for the remission of our sins. It was all part of the journey to fulfil His purpose.

"He was oppressed, and he was afflicted yet he opened not his mouth: he is brought as a lamb to the slaughter, and as a sheep before her shearers is dumb, so he openeth not his mouth" (Isaiah 53:7).

Instead He said, "Father, forgive them; for they know not what they do" (Luke 23:34).

He petitioned God to forgive the perpetrators despite the suffering He endured.

Another character in the Bible who showed forgiveness was Joseph. His brothers despised him because he was the favourite son of Jacob. They planned to kill him, but his elder brother Reuben convinced them to spare him.

Joseph was placed in a pit and then sold to merchants. He was betrayed by his own flesh and blood. When he became governor of Egypt, his brothers came to buy corn. He tested them to see whether they were the same way.

Joseph showed kindness to them after he realised they had changed. Through all the turmoil he faced, being betrayed, separated from his family, and sold into slavery, he still found it in his heart to forgive his brothers. He did not throw them into prison, but he reunited with them.

Joseph beckoned his brothers to come near to him, and he revealed himself to them. This demonstrated his forgiveness. He also asked about their father. He invited them to live in Egypt so they would have provisions during the famine.

Here, we learn that forgiveness is important to mend relations, just as in the parable of the prodigal son in Luke 15. The younger son took his share of inheritance and left. He squandered it and was left without. There was also a famine in that place. Therefore, he decided to return home and seek forgiveness from his father, and he apologised to him. He intended to work as a servant in his father's house.

However, when he was yet in the distance, the father saw him and was overjoyed. He warmly and openly welcomed his younger son. He called for a grand feast and requested the best robe be put on him, a ring be put on his hand, and shoes be put on his feet. This indicated that the father had forgiven him no matter the circumstances. This also signifies that God is willing to accept anyone who comes to Him repentant of their sins. He is willing to forgive.

"Come now, and let us reason together, saith the Lord: though your sins be as scarlet, they shall be as white as snow; though they be red like crimson, they shall be as wool" (Isaiah 1:18).

Prayer of Forgiveness

Heavenly Father,
I bow before You,
Humbly asking Your forgiveness.
I seek remission of my sins.
Cleanse my heart of all impurities
So that I can serve
You wholeheartedly.
Teach me to walk in Your ways.
Let Your words be a lamp
Unto my feet and
A light unto my path.
May I forgive those
Who have been unjust to me.
Just as You forgive, Lord
Help me also to forgive.
Hear this, my prayer,
In the beloved name
Of our Lord and Saviour
Jesus Christ.

Amen.

Healing

But he was wounded for our transgressions, he
was bruised for our iniquities: the chastisement
of our peace was upon him; and with his stripes
we are healed.

(Isaiah 53:5)

Healing is the process of letting go. Healing means you
have forgiven and freed yourself of bitterness, anger,
resentment, betrayal, and hurt. It means you have
relinquished the negative emotions that were dominant
in your heart and mind. The longer you hold on to hurt,
the longer you will take to heal.

Forgiveness brings healing to you in all dimensions
emotionally, physically, and psychologically. It improves
your overall health. Negative emotions are replaced with
harmony and wholeness.

Healing begins when you start to nurture yourself
with love and care. It is loving yourself enough to choose
peacefulness in your life. Self-love and self-care are of
paramount importance for the process of healing.

Being healed renews positivity in your life and reduces stress. When you are healed from the hurt of your past, you are able to fulfil your purpose. This is possible because you can see things in better perspectives. Your heart and mind are free and receptive to positive things.

Healing can be brought about by being creative and doing the things you enjoy the most. Your talents and skills are pivotal in this process. Listening to music also helps to heal. David was called to play the harp for King Saul so he would be healed.

Nature also works wonders for healing. Creation works in tandem for our well-being. It brings you to a place of serenity. The sights, sounds, and elements are unique and provide immeasurable doses of healing. If you take the time to appreciate the environment, you will find the peace you desire.

However, the true physician for healing is Almighty God. When you open your heart and surrender all to Him, then you can be truly healed.

"The Lord is nigh unto them that are of a broken heart; and saveth such as be of a contrite spirit" (Psalm 34:18).

His love is sufficient to mend brokenness and make whole again. Placing your trust in Him guarantees this. God's words provide comfort and are the best medicine for healing. They also encourage and strengthen. During times of trials and despair, you can rely on His words to see you through.

Joseph, the governor of Egypt, faced adversity and betrayal by his brethren but forgave them. This was an imperative stage in his life. Joseph forgiving them for their actions meant the removal of bitterness and anger. This brought healing, peace, and blessings to him. This is evident by the birth of his sons.

> And Joseph called the name of the firstborn Manasseh: For God, said he, hath made me forget all my toil, and all my father's house.

> And the name of the second called he Ephraim: For God hath caused me to be fruitful in the land of my affliction.

> (Genesis 41:51–52)

He indicated to his brethren that it was God's plan for him to preserve life, be a deliverer, and save their lives. His struggles, inner strength, and forgiveness can be equated to that of the Lord Jesus Christ. They both endured these stages in their lives before fulfilling their purposes.

King David called out to God for remission of his sins. He implored healing and cleansing. He urged God to make him whole again and mend his brokenness. He showed his remorse for adultery, and God forgave and healed him, allowing him to fulfil his purpose.

> Purge me with hyssop, and I shall be clean: wash me, and I shall be whiter than snow.

> Make me to hear joy and gladness; that the bones which thou hast broken may rejoice.

Hide thy face from my sins, and blot out all mine iniquities.

Create in me a clean heart, O God; and renew a right spirit within me.

Cast me not away from thy presence; and take not thy Holy Spirit from me.

(Psalm 51:7–11)

The Apostle Paul, previously called Saul, was blind for three days. This was like the Lord's death and resurrection after three days. It symbolised death to his old way of life. No longer would Paul persecute the Christians. The return of his sight was healing, awakening, and vision for a new life. He was forgiven and fulfilled God's purpose: to spread the message of the good news of the Lord Jesus Christ.

Prayer for Healing

God of Abraham, Isaac, and Jacob,
I pray for healing today.
May You search me
And enlighten what is dark within.
May You bring healing
And mend all brokenness,
Sadness, and agony.
May I be healed
Mentally, emotionally,
Physically, and spiritually.
You are the greatest physician,
The greatest healer.
I have faith and trust in You
That I will be whole again
In the beloved name
Of our dear Lord Jesus.

Amen.

Restoration

But the God of all grace, who hath called us
unto his eternal glory by Christ Jesus, after that
ye have suffered a while, make you perfect,
stablish, strengthen, settle you.

To him be glory and dominion for ever and
ever. Amen.

(1 Peter 5:10–11)

Restoration is a repairing of something, to bring it back
like it was before. In the Bible, it signifies hope and
abundance. When God restores, it is better than it was
previously.

Inner strength initiates inner peace; inner peace brings
forgiveness and healing; healing fosters restoration.

We learn that Joseph forgave his brothers, and he was
healed and restored. David was forgiven by God, and he
was healed and restored. Ruth, through her resilience
and faith, was healed and restored. Job, through his
perseverance and trust in God, was healed and restored.
The prodigal son was forgiven by his father and was

restored. Paul was forgiven by God, and his sight was restored. All for fulfilling God's purpose.

King David also pleaded for God's restoration in Psalm 51:12–15.

> Restore unto me the joy of thy salvation; and uphold me with thy free spirit.

> Then will I teach transgressors thy ways; and sinners shall be converted unto thee.

> Deliver me from bloodguiltiness, O God, thou God of my salvation: and my tongue shall sing aloud of thy righteousness.

> O Lord, open thou my lips; and my mouth shall shew forth thy praise.

Throughout the course of history, the nation of Israel committed sins before God. He was so exhausted of their wickedness and declared unto Jeremiah the prophet that he would slay them in his anger and wrath; dead bodies would fill the houses and palaces. The city would become desolate.

"For this city hath been to me as a provocation of mine anger and of my fury from the day that they built it even unto this day; that I should remove it from before my face" (Jeremiah 32:31).

However, God demonstrated His love for this nation and forgave them.

Behold, I will gather them out of all countries, whither I have driven them in mine anger and in my fury and in great wrath; and I will bring them again unto this place, and I will cause them do dwell safely:

And they shall be my people, and I will be their God.

(Jeremiah 32:37–38)

He also promised to bring healing to His people after forgiving them. "Behold, I will bring health and cure, and I will cure them, and will reveal unto them the abundance of peace and truth" (Jeremiah 33:6).

God was intent on restoring them even though they did wrong. He assured them of healing, and ultimately he would restore.

And I will bring again the captivity of my people of Israel, and they shall build the waste cities and inhabit them; and they shall plant vineyards and drink the wine thereof; and they shall also make gardens, and eat the fruit of them.

And I will plant them upon their land, and they shall no more be pulled up out of their land which I have given them, saith the Lord thy God. (Amos 9:14–15)

Just like the others who forgave or were forgiven, were healed, fulfilled their purposes, and were restored, God has a purpose for Israel.

He forgives and will bring healing and restoration to them so His purpose will be fulfilled. That is for the Lord Jesus Christ to be made the Eternal King. He will bring peace and rule over all the earth from Jerusalem, which means "City of Peace". It is also rightly dubbed the "City of the Great King".

> Behold the days come, saith the Lord that I will raise unto David a righteous Branch, and a King shall reign and prosper, and shall execute judgment and justice in the earth.

> In his days Judah shall be saved and Israel shall dwell safely: and this is his name whereby he shall be called, THE LORD OUR RIGHTEOUSNESS.

> (Jeremiah 23:5–6)

Prayer for Restoration

Beloved Father in heaven,
I implore restoration in my life
That my joy and happiness
Will return, O Lord.
May I be filled
With Your peace,
Strength, comfort,
And hope once again.
May whatever has been
Taken from me
Be restored sevenfold.
May Your hands always be open
To pour Your blessings
Over my life
In the sweet name of Jesus,
Our Redeemer.

Amen.

Conclusion

By tapping into your inner strength, you can overcome life's challenges. Have fortitude and let the light within illuminate your path to inner peace, forgiveness, and healing.

Be at peace with others. Seek forgiveness from God for your mistakes, and forgive others. All of this is for the greater good of fulfilling your purpose, and ultimately you will be restored.

Allow the fruits of the spirit to build your inner strength. "Love, joy, peace, longsuffering, gentleness, goodness, faith, meekness and temperance" (Galatians 5:22–23).

God always wants to restore us and has a purpose for each of us to fulfil. He desires that we come to Him with faithful and pure hearts. So trust Him and listen to His voice.

"For I know the thoughts I think toward you, saith the Lord, thoughts of peace and not of evil, to give you an expected end" (Jeremiah 29:11).

Let It Shine

There is a light within
To enhance this journey
You are travelling.
It is the courage you possess,
Your inner strength,
Willpower, and resilience.
So when you are in despair,
Tap into it, and
You will overcome all fears.
Challenges you may face
Are temporary.
With inner strength,
You will gain the victory.
So let that light illuminate,
And you will see
The hand of fate.

Bless the Lord,
O my soul:
And all that is within me,
Bless His Holy Name.
Bless the Lord,
O my soul,
And forget not
All his benefits.

—Psalm 103:1–2

Printed in the United States
by Baker & Taylor Publisher Services